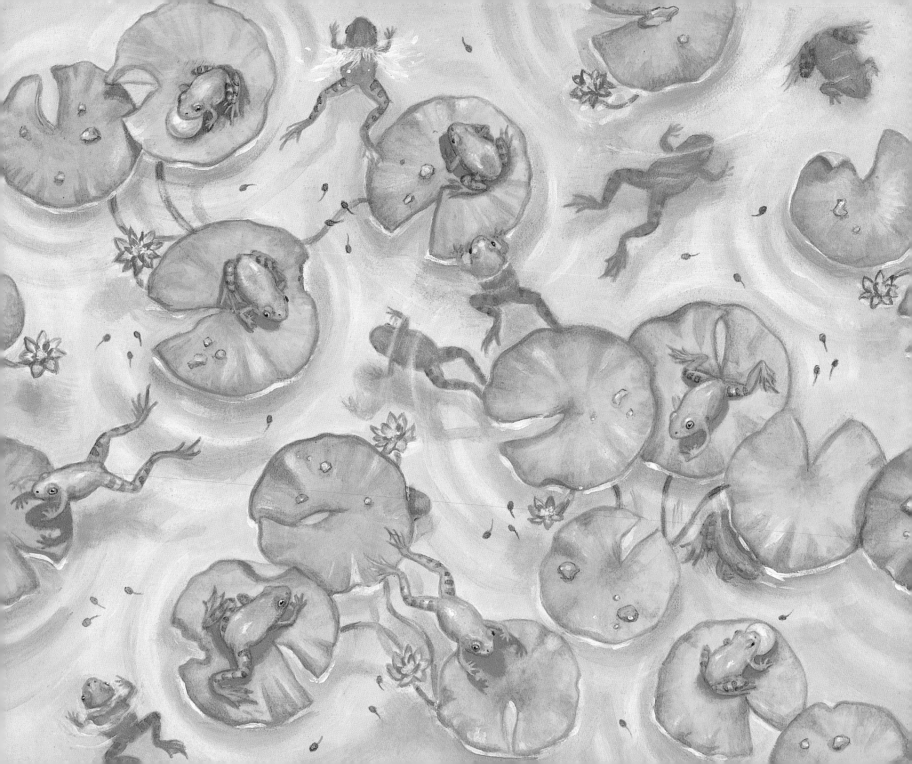

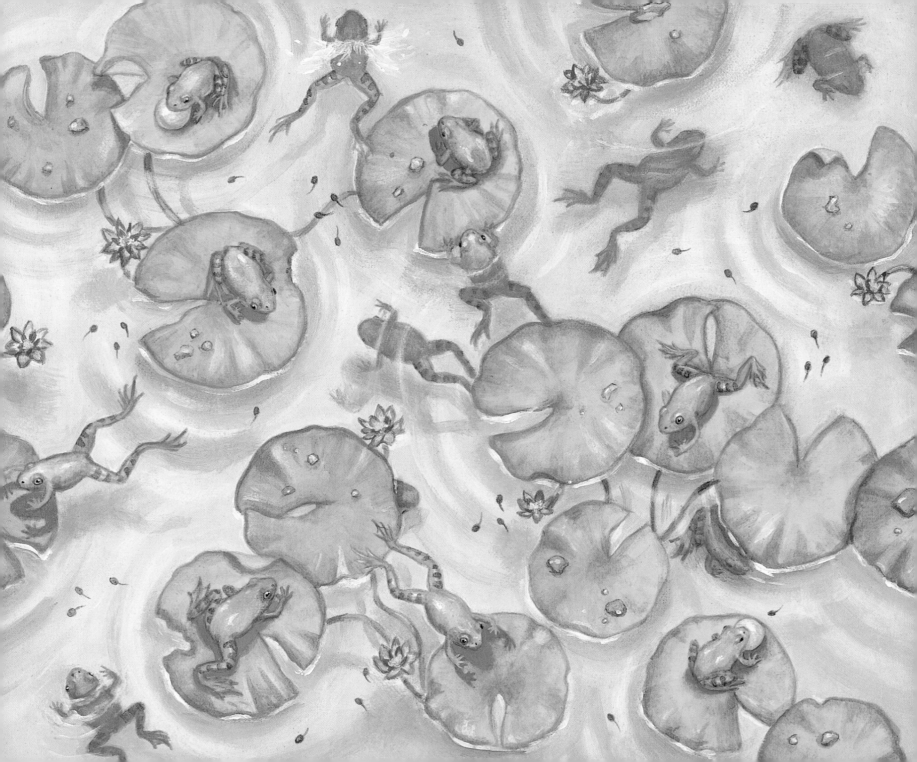

LET'S-READ-AND-FIND-OUT SCIENCE®

Why Frogs Are
WET

STAGE 2

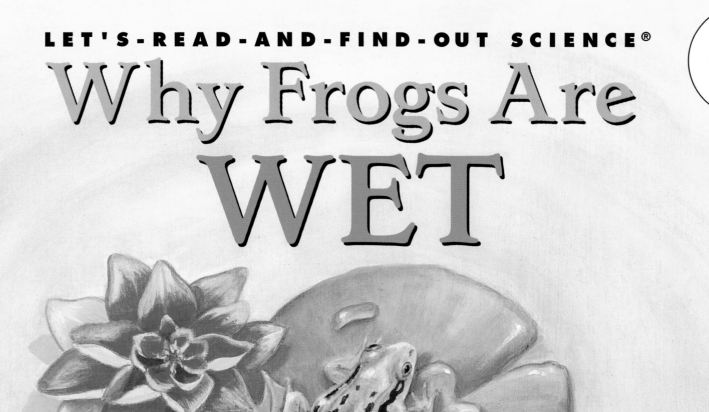

by Judy Hawes • illustrated by Mary Ann Fraser

HarperCollinsPublishers

Pine Barrens Tree Frog

For Eric Damon
–M.A.F.

Special thanks to Valerie Chase
of the National Aquarium of Baltimore
for her time and expert review

The art for this book was created in acrylic.

The Let's-Read-and-Find-Out Science book series was originated by Dr. Franklyn M. Branley, Astronomer Emeritus and former Chairman of the American Museum–Hayden Planetarium, and was formerly co-edited by him and Dr. Roma Gans, Professor Emeritus of Childhood Education, Teachers College, Columbia University. Text and illustrations for each of the books in the series are checked for accuracy by an expert in the relevant field. For information address HarperCollins Children's Books, a division of HarperCollins Publishers, 195 Broadway, New York, NY 10007. or visit our web site at www.harperchildrens.com.

HarperCollins®, ■®, and Let's Read-and-Find-Out Science® are trademarks of HarperCollins Publishers Inc.

Why Frogs Are Wet
Text copyright © 1968 by Judith Hawes
Text copyright renewed 1996 by Judith Hawes
Illustrations copyright © 2000 by Mary Ann Fraser
Manufactured in China. All rights reserved.

Library of Congress Cataloging-in-Publication Data
Hawes, Judy.
   Why frogs are wet / by Judy Hawes ; illustrated by Mary Ann Fraser
   Published: New York : HarperCollins Publishers, 2000.
      p.   cm. – (Let's-read-and-find-out science.   Stage 2)
   Notes: Originally published : New York : T.Y. Crowell Co., 1968, in series: Let's-read-and-find-out science book.
   Summary: A brief study of the first creatures on earth to develop voices and an aversion to dry skin.
   ISBN 0-06-028161-8. – ISBN 0-06-028162-6 (lib. bdg.)
   ISBN 0-06-445195-X (pbk.)
   1. Frogs–Juvenile literature.   [1. Frogs.]   I. Fraser, Mary Ann, ill.   II. Title.   III. Series.
QL668.E2H335   2000   98-44340
597.8'289 21   AC

Typography by Elynn Cohen   ❖   15 SCP 21 20 19
Newly Illustrated Edition

Why Frogs Are
WET

Chaco Leaf Frog

Frogs were here on earth before people. They were here before monkeys, or cats. Frogs were here before giraffes. Frogs have been here for millions of years.

Long before there were frogs, there were fish. The fish breathed through their gills. After a long time, new kinds of fish appeared. These new fish had lungs for breathing. They could live out of water for a little while. When their ponds dried up, they were able to flop about on land. They had to flop, because they had no legs.

Later, some kinds of fish appeared that had legs in place of fins. Now they could move on land or in the water. These were forefathers of our frogs.

7

A frog can live in the water and on the land. It is called an "amphibian." "Amphibian" is from a Greek phrase that means "having a double life."

The frog has wet skin. The wet skin holds the secret of its double life. The frog breathes through its skin. It also breathes through its lungs.

Green Frogs

Northern
Leopard Frog

Underwater a frog breathes through its skin. It gets air out of the water. On land a frog breathes through its lungs and its skin. But it can breathe through its skin only when the skin is wet. It cannot get enough air through its lungs alone. If the skin dries out, the frog cannot breathe. The frog dies.

A frog's skin is always fresh. It sheds its skin often.
New, wet skin has already grown under the old.
The frog eats the old skin.

European Common Frog

In the fall and winter frogs dig into the mud under streams and ponds. They stay there for months and months. They hardly breathe, and their hearts slow down. They hibernate.

As soon as frogs come out in the spring from their hibernation, they hunt for mates.

Carpenter Frog

Eastern Wood Frogs

Some kinds of frogs live all their lives in water. Others live in damp woods or marshland. But all frogs return to lakes, ponds, or puddles to mate and lay their eggs. The female frogs lay their eggs in the water. Then the male frogs fertilize the eggs.

A clump of eggs looks like a large helping of tapioca pudding. The eggs hatch in four to twenty-one days. Frog babies, just hatched, are called tadpoles or polliwogs. They look and swim like fish. They breathe through gills like fish.

The gills look like fingers on either side of the tadpole's head. After a few days the gills are covered over with skin. Then you can see hind legs growing. Next the front legs appear. The tail is slowly taken into the body. Lungs for breathing on land grow inside the frog. Now the little frog is an amphibian. It can live on land or in the water.

15

Blue Poison Dart Frog
Surinam
The male carries the eggs
and tadpoles on his back
until they are well developed.

Glass Frog
Costa Rica
These frogs are
transparent underneath.

Common Gray Tree Frog
North America
This frog changes color according
to its mood. It may be gray, green,
or brown.

White's Tree Frog
Australia
This frog is often found
in people's bathrooms.

Arum Frog
Southern Africa
This frog is ivory when
the ivory swamp lilies are
in bloom. The rest of the
year it is brown with silvery
stripes along its sides.

There are more than two thousand kinds of frogs.
They are found all over the world. All of them have
wet skin. Many frogs are green or brown, but there
are frogs of almost every color.

Poison Dart Frog
Colombia
This is the most poisonous
frog in the world.

Darwin's Frog
Chile
This frog floats upside down in
the water to imitate a fallen leaf.

Painted Reed Frog
Tanzania to South Africa
During warm months hundreds
of these frogs call with a series
of shrill whistles.

Tomato Frog
Madagascar
The tomato frog spends most
of the year in hiding, but comes
out during spring rains.

Asian Horned Frog
Southern Asia
This frog looks like a brown leaf
on the forest floor.

There are big frogs and little frogs.
A giant frog lives in Africa.
It is twelve inches long,
not counting its legs.
   The largest frog in
America is the bullfrog.
Its body is six to eight
inches long. The smallest
frog in America is a tree frog
called a Little Grass Frog.
It is only half an inch long.

Actual sizes

Goliath Frog

Bullfrog

Little Grass Frog

19

Frogs were some of the first creatures on earth to
have voices. They use them when they hunt for mates
in the spring. When a frog sings, its throat looks like a
blown-up balloon. The voices of bullfrogs are deep and
low. They seem to say "jug o' rum!" Tree frogs have a
high-pitched song. It rings like distant bells. Other
frog calls are grunts, squeaks, or squawks. Most
female frogs do not sing, but they scream when
they are frightened.

Mink Frog

Spring Peepers

Southern Cricket Frog

Frogs are great jumpers. They can leap
ten, twenty, or thirty times their body length.
They jump very fast and in zigzags.
   The frog jumps to get away from its enemies.
Sometimes it jumps to catch its food.

When it looks for food, the frog does not jump about carelessly. It usually waits, motionless, for insects to fly within striking distance. It may sit on a branch, a lily pad, or a rock, or it may float in the water.

Its big, bulging eyes can see in all directions. Frogs stare without blinking. They can protect their eyes from drying by shutting them halfway. They can still see, because they can look right through their lower eyelids.

African Bullfrog

Pickerel Frog

26

Frogs will eat anything that seems to be a living, moving insect. If the insect stops moving, the frog will pay no attention to it. Frogs will starve before they eat dead bugs.

When the frog's staring eyes spot a victim within striking distance, the frog's tongue makes the catch. It seldom misses.

A frog's tongue is different from ours.
It is attached to the front of its mouth.
It folds back toward its throat.
    As a frog jumps for an insect,
its tongue flips forward.
The far end of the tongue has
a sticky surface.

Red-legged Frogs

This sticky end wraps around the insect. The insect sticks to the tongue, and the tongue swings back into the frog's mouth. The frog throws the insect down its throat. All this takes less than a tenth of a second.

Frogs catch insects that are in water, in the air, or on land. They come out to find food at twilight or on rainy and cloudy days. During the heat of the day they hide under damp leaves or under the water. They have to keep their skin wet because they are amphibians.

Never forget that frogs are amphibians.
They can live in the water or on land.
But only as long as their skin stays wet!

What do frog eggs feel like?

To find out, you will need:

1 egg	a handful of large pearl tapioca
small pot	clock, watch, or timer
cooking tongs	spoon
2 bowls of water	

Cooked tapioca feels like frog eggs. How would frog eggs feel compared to a chicken egg?

1. Have an adult help you boil the egg.
2. When it is done, turn off the heat and carefully remove the egg from the pot with the cooking tongs. Put the egg into one bowl of water.
3. Put a handful of large pearl tapioca into the pot, bring the water back to a boil, and let it boil for 15 minutes.
4. Turn off the heat, and have an adult help you carefully spoon the tapioca into the other bowl of water.
5. Wait for 5 minutes, and then touch the tapioca and the egg. How are they different?

If a frog doesn't keep its skin wet, it will die. Frog eggs have to stay wet too. What happens when frog eggs are taken out of the water? To find out, carefully pour out the water in each bowl until only the tapioca and the egg are left.

1. After an hour, touch the tapioca. What does it feel like? Now touch the egg. Does it feel different?
2. Touch them again after two or three hours. Now how do they feel?
3. Let the tapioca and the egg sit overnight. Touch them again in the morning. How has each changed?

Read More About Frogs

You can learn more about frogs in these great books:

From Tadpole to Frog by Wendy Pfeffer, illustrated by Holly Keller

Red-Eyed Tree Frog by Joy Cowley, photographs by Nic Bishop

A New Frog by Pamela Hickman, illustrated by Heather Collins

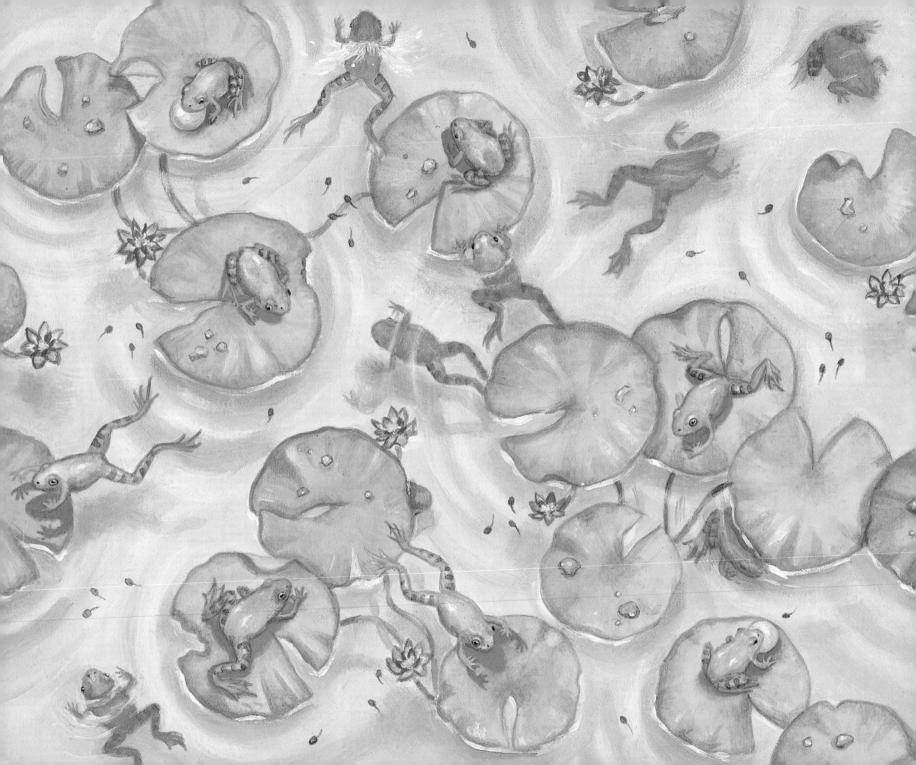

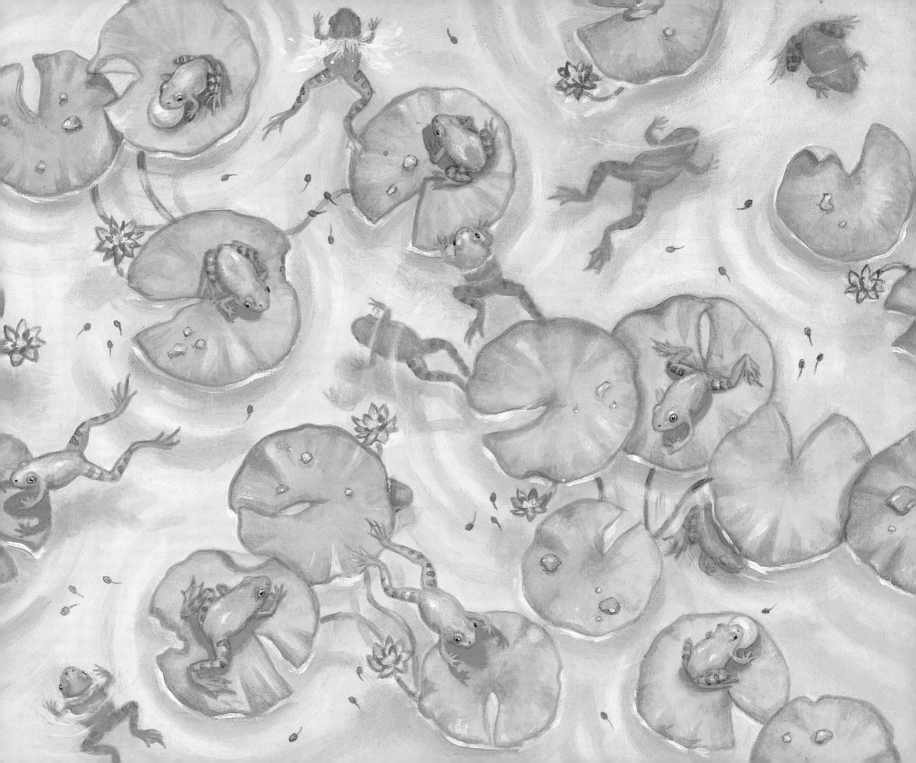